Peace Be With You All

Peace Be With You All

100 Sayings by Pope Leo XIV

Edited by
Matthias Kopp

Published in the United States by New City Press
136 Madison Avenue, Floors 5 & 6, PMB #4290
New York, NY 10016
www.newcitypress.com

Translated by the New City Press editorial staff from the original German edition, *Der Friede Sei Mit Euch Allen: 100 Worte von Papst Leo XIV*

Cover photo: Dreamstime

ISBN 978-1-56548-732-1 (Print)
ISBN 978-1-56548-733-8 (E-book)

Library of Congress Control Number: 2025947891

Printed in the United States of America

Contents

Introduction

When Pope Francis died on Easter Monday, April 21, 2025, the world seemed to stand still for a moment. He could hardly have chosen a more impressive date for his passing into heaven, as the Gospel of the disciples of Emmaus is read on this day, they who "recognized" the Lord at the end of their journey. In the days that followed, the world bowed its head to Francis, who was rightly honored as the conscience of the world.

The funeral ceremonies, on April 26, 2025, marked the beginning of a long pre-conclave, which was initially characterized in particular by the nine days of mourning following the funeral. The daily services in St. Peter's Basilica played a role in this, as did the gradual gathering of (almost) all cardinals—those eligible to vote and those over eighty years of age—who gathered for talks, discussions, and to paint a comprehensive picture of the state of the Church worldwide and in Rome. A central part of the deliberations was the profile that the future pope would need to have.

The period leading up to the start of the conclave generated even greater media interest than during the 2013 papal election and was certainly comparable to that seen in 2005. No fewer than 6,500 journalists were accredited by the Vatican. In front of St. Peter's Square and along the entire boulevard leading to Castel Sant'Angelo, the Via della Conciliazione, there was hardly a square foot that was not occupied by reporters.

There were long broadcasts on public radio . . . and on private providers almost every day; thus, the waiting period became a Church media event of unprecedented proportions—and worldwide at that. The Catholic Church is still a source of fascination for many people, even for media outlets that have little to do with the Church. The fact that in the 21st century—in the midst of the digital world and artificial intelligence—an institution communicates with smoke signals, at such an important moment as the papal election, is just as impressive as the gaze of millions of people worldwide on the rusty stovepipe that the

Vatican fire brigade installed with acrobatic finesse on the roof of the Sistine Chapel.

When a pair of seagulls strut up and down this chimney, they turned out to be the best entertainers to help pass the time while waiting. This gradually became almost unbearable, especially for the journalists: At some point, they ran out of people to talk to and started interviewing themselves. This was a sign that it was time: We needed a new pope.

The summer weather in Rome, on May 8, 2025, bathed St. Peter's Basilica in a spot-light-like backlight for the camera crews. It was difficult to make out the first wisps of white smoke from the seagull chimney. But soon, at 6:08 p.m., the bells of St. Peter's provided certainty: *Habemus papam!*

It would take a whole hour before the world would know who he was. For weeks, there had been speculation; betting offices had been set up, and experts and less knowledgeable individuals in Roman cafés and restaurants thought they knew who would win the "race." Well-known and not a few self-appointed Vatican experts speculated about the 133 names of the cardinals, almost every one of whom had at some point been considered "*papabile*." It was also notable which cardinals positioned themselves in interviews immediately before the conclave.

And once again, as in 2013, the world was astonished when Cardinal Protodeacon Dominique Mamberti announced the new pope at 7:13 p.m., a choice that few had anticipated: Cardinal Robert Francis Prevost, who took the name Leo XIV—an American and Augustinian monk, a cardinal of the Curia, and Andean bishop on the papal throne.

There stood the new pope, amid the cheers of tens of thousands of people on the loggia of St. Peter's: smiling and inwardly moved, the man with a meteoric career, who just a few weeks earlier had moved into a new apartment in the palace of the Congregation for the Doctrine of the Faith, where the nameplate on the doorbell read "Card. Prevost." Above all, there was no imitation of Pope Francis to be seen on the balcony. The historic stole, which Francis had rejected, had been put on by Leo, who had jotted down his first address as a sketch in a college notebook. Whereas, in 2013, it was "*Buona sera*," Leo XIV's first words expressed his inner conviction and ultimately a keyword of his program to the faithful: "Peace be with you all! This is the first greeting of the risen Christ, the Good Shepherd, who gave his life for the flock of God. I, too, wish that this greeting of peace may enter your hearts, reach your families, all people, wherever they may be, all peoples, the whole earth. Peace be with you! It is the peace of the risen Christ. A peace that is unarmed and disarming, humble and persevering. A peace that comes from God, the God who loves us all, unconditionally."

The speech on the loggia set the tone. And in the very first days of his pontificate, Leo XIV made it clear that he wanted to use every peaceful political option in the world by offering spaces for dialogue through his diplomacy—that of the Holy See. This was evident at his inauguration, on May 18, 2025, when the world, after the funeral of Francis, traveled to Rome once again: Heads of state and government, crowned heads, and diplomatic representatives, but above all, ordinary believers wanted to pay their respects to the new pope. Leo can now build on these contacts, especially when it comes to (world) political or humanitarian issues.

The Vatican had to adjust to a new, much younger pope who sets a brisk pace, takes spontaneous trips in a minivan, and holds up to ten official audiences every day. Like Francis, he also seeks to meet people wherever possible. His entourage, from security to his personal staff, often has to take a deep breath. At the same time, Leo XIV knows how to use the existing apparatus as a working tool; he consults with the Secretariat of State and the dicasteries, as evidenced by his own experience as Prefect of the Dicastery for Bishops, which he headed for two years. Many in the Curia say that the pope has already settled into his office after just a few weeks. In fact, one senses that he enjoys it. Of course, the papacy is a heavy load, but Leo XIV does not give the slightest impression that it is a burden. He accepted the office, and when he did so, it was clear to him: Now he has to fulfill this office as a bridge builder into the world.

For the pope, one thing remains clear: He is "a humble worker in the Lord's vineyard," but one who can and wants to govern and organize, argue theologically and act pastorally. "I was chosen without any merit of my own and come to you with fear and trembling as a brother who wants to make himself a servant of your faith and your joy and walk with you on the path of God's love, who wants us all to be one family," said Leo on the day of his inauguration, on May 18, 2025. This expresses something about how he understands his ministry and how he wants to exercise it: in cooperation, and not in singular decision-making. Without using the word at this point, something of Leo XIV's synodal thinking is evident here. He witnessed the two sessions of the World Synod on Synodality in 2023 and 2024 at the Vatican. His thoughtfulness is reflected in his first speeches on synodality: continuing on the path, together and courageously, respecting the cultural contexts in the respective countries, and always keeping the whole Church in view.

Leo XIV cannot be pigeonholed. His long stay in Peru, his American origins, his responsibility as head of the Augustinian order on five continents, and his experience in the Curia have made him a cosmopolitan. It would be wrong to describe him as "the American" or "the Peruvian"; Leo is more than that and has ultimately always been at home in the world. Speaking on May 16, 2025, to the diplomatic corps of ambassadors accredited to the Holy See, he said: "In a way, my own life experience, which has unfolded between North America, South America, and Europe, is representative of this desire to cross borders in order to encounter different people and cultures." This is precisely who Leo XIV, formerly Cardinal Prevost, is: a person who wants to encounter others, who above all wants to understand others, and who, even before the beginning of his pontificate, in many ways, was a bridge builder, whether in his Peruvian diocese, in his religious community, or as Prefect of the Dicastery for Bishops, where for example he played a key role in facilitating understanding between representatives of the German Bishops' Conference and the Roman Bishops' Conference during high-level talks in 2024.

What distinguishes the new pope? Here, one observation may be permitted based on experience with him as a religious, bishop, and cardinal. Prevost is someone who is an excellent listener, who is undoubtedly a "decisionista"—a decision-maker—not someone who waits things out, nor someone who makes quick and off-the-cuff decisions, but rather someone who acts in a thoughtful, reflective, and prayerful manner. He is a personality who is always well prepared for conversations. As an example, because it shows a detail, I recall a meeting with twenty-five journalists from the Society of Catholic Publicists, which I was able to arrange on January 5, 2024. A colleague asked about the upcoming bishop election in Rottenburg-Stuttgart (Germany). It is astonishing that Cardinal Prevost, without knowing that such a question would be asked, was able to explain to the astonished group of media representatives the details of the concordat applicable there. And this is how bishops of the Universal Church, colleagues, and heads of state experience him today: extremely well prepared.

Pope Leo XIV sets further milestones in his still young pontificate. The first ecumenical encounters, several of them with the honorary head of world Orthodoxy, Patriarch Bartholomew I of Constantinople, and the talks with representatives of world religions indicate that the cosmopolitan Leo will build on the experiences in dialogue from his previous biography: to learn from each other, to listen to each other, and to walk together on a path in this world.

The pope feels connected to this world, and in the aforementioned speech to the diplomatic corps, he added, "My own story is that of a citizen, a descendant of immigrants, who is himself an emigrant." There is hardly a better way to describe the concept of a citizen of the world. This is another reason why Leo will focus on the issue of migration and emigration. At the same time, he is aware of the pastoral discontinuities in Europe and North America and the pastoral beginnings in Africa and Asia. As Pope of the Universal Church, he will perceive the regional differences and integrate them into the teaching of his pontificate.

To this, he joins his own theological hermeneutics of understanding and a remarkable organizational approach to action. At the same time, Leo XIV never tires of reminding us, in almost every address, of his predecessor Francis, which shows that he sees himself in continuity with him, but which does not mean that he does not develop his own profile.

This profile is particularly evident in his name and in his episcopal—and now papal—motto: "The Christians themselves with their head . . . are One Christ. Not He One and we many, but we, the many, in Him One. One man, therefore, Christ, head and body. What is his body? His Church."* This means that even though we Christians are many, we are one in *the one* Christ. This idea of unity is formative for Bishop and Cardinal Prevost, and also for Leo XIV, because he is concerned with the whole in Christ.

---

* *"Ipsi christiani cum capite suo—unus est Christus; non ille unus et nos multi, sed et nos multi in illo unum. Unus ergo homo Christus, caput et corpus? Ecclesia eius . . ."* (*Corpus Christianorum* Series Latina XL, 1869).

Thus, the words of Augustine are to be understood ecclesiologically, which is why the pope also makes it clear that he understands his ministry as Christ's representative for all, as he emphasized during the Mass for taking possession of the Lateran Basilica, on May 25, 2025: "For my part, I would like to express my firm desire to contribute to this great ongoing process by listening to everyone as much as possible, in order to learn, understand and decide things together, as Saint Augustine would say, 'as a Christian with you and a Bishop for you' (cf. *Sermo 340*, 1). I ask you to help me in this with your prayers and your love, mindful of the words of St. Leo the Great: 'All the good we accomplish in our ministry is the work of Christ; not ours, for without him we can do nothing; but we boast of him, from whom all the effectiveness of our actions comes' (*Sermo 5, de natali ipsius*, 4)."

The name chosen by Cardinal Prevost also attests to the effectiveness of his actions: Leo XIV. The reference to his predecessor Leo XIII (1878–1903) is unmistakable, especially in view of the latter's social encyclical *Rerum novarum,* of May 15, 1891, with which he laid the foundation for Catholic social teaching. The new pope explained to the cardinals, on May 10, 2025, in an address: "Precisely because I feel called to continue on this path, I have decided to take the name Leo XIV. There are several reasons for this, but first and foremost, because Pope Leo XIII addressed the social question in connection with the first great industrial revolution. And today, the Church offers everyone the treasure of its social teaching in order to respond to another industrial revolution and to the developments in artificial intelligence, which bring new challenges with regard to the defense of human dignity, justice, and work." And on the day of his inauguration, Leo XIV once again referred to his namesake predecessor, at the same time programmatically reiterating what he had emphasized on the day of his election: peace. "Brothers and sisters. This is the hour for love! The heart of the Gospel is the love of God that makes us brothers and sisters, and with my predecessor Leo XIII, we can ask ourselves today: If this criterion were to prevail in the world, would not every dispute immediately cease and peace be restored?" (Encyclical *Rerum novarum*, 21).

There are still many surprises to be discovered about Pope Leo XIV. With his gestures and encounters, with his words and texts, he touches the hearts of people. 100 Sayings have been selected in this anthology for the beginning of his pontificate, from the first one hundred days. Many more words will follow, and many gestures. The one hundred sayings presented here can help us better understand Leo XIV. They are words of guidance and encouragement for our own journey through life. They are the words of a pope who wants to meet people and who, in the end, appeals to each and every one of us personally, as he did on July 5, 2025: "Listen to your heart!"

Matthias Kopp

100 Sayings by
Pope Leo XIV

Peace be with you all! . . .
It is the peace
of the risen Christ.
A peace that is
unarmed and disarming,
humble and persevering.
A peace that comes from God,
the God who loves us all,
unconditionally.

God loves us;
God loves you all,
and evil will not prevail!

All too often we consider [peace] a "negative" word, indicative only of the absence of war and conflict, since opposition is a perennial part of human nature, frequently leading us to live in a constant "state of conflict" at home, at work, and in society. Peace then appears simply as a respite, a pause between one dispute and another, given that, no matter how hard we try, tensions will always be present, a little like embers burning beneath the ashes, ready to ignite at any moment.

Working for peace
requires acting justly.

* * *

The path to peace demands hearts and minds trained in concern for others and capable of perceiving the common good in today's world. For the road to peace involves everyone and leads to the fostering of right relationships between all living beings.

All too much violence exists
in the world and our societies.
Amid wars, terrorism,
human trafficking,
and widespread aggression,
our children and young people
need to be able to experience
the culture of life, dialogue,
and mutual respect.

If you want peace,
prepare
institutions of peace.

Whenever those
who have suffered
injustice and violence
resist the temptation
to seek revenge,
they become the most
credible agents
of nonviolent peacebuilding
processes. Nonviolence,
as a method and a style,
must distinguish our decisions,
our relationships, and our actions.

From a Christian perspective but also in other religious traditions peace is first and foremost a gift. It is the first gift of Christ: "My peace I give to you" (Jn 14:27). Yet it is an active and demanding gift. It engages and challenges each of us, regardless of our cultural background or religious affiliation, demanding first of all that we work on ourselves.

Only a peaceful heart can spread
peace in the family, society,
and international relations.
May the Spirit of the risen Christ
open paths of reconciliation
wherever there is war;
may he enlighten those who govern
and give them the courage
to make gestures of de-escalation
and dialogue.

Peace is built in the heart
and from the heart,
by eliminating pride and
vindictiveness and
carefully choosing our words.
For words, too,
—not only weapons—
can wound and even kill.

Peace
begins with each one of us:
in the way we look at others,
listen to others,
and speak about others.
In this sense,
the way we communicate
is of fundamental importance:
We must say "no"
to the war of words and images;
we must reject the paradigm of war.

This is a Beatitude that challenges all of us, but it is particularly relevant to you, calling each one of you to strive for a different kind of communication, one that does not seek consensus at all costs, does not use aggressive words, does not follow the culture of competition, and never separates the search for truth from the love with which we must humbly seek it.

Let us disarm words,
and we will help
to disarm the world.

Disarmed and disarming
communication allows us to share
a different view of the world
and to act in a manner
consistent with our human dignity.

No one is exempted
from striving to ensure respect
for the dignity of every person,
especially the most
frail and vulnerable,
from the unborn to the elderly,
from the sick to the unemployed,
citizens and immigrants alike.

All of us, in the course of our lives, can find ourselves healthy or sick, employed or unemployed, living in our native land or in a foreign country, yet our dignity always remains unchanged:

It is the dignity of a creature willed and loved by God.

The Church must face the challenges posed by the times.

We are incarnate
in time and history,
since God chose
the human condition
and the languages of humanity.
The Church, therefore,
is called to follow the same path,
in order that the joy of the Gospel
may reach everyone,
mediated through today's cultures
and languages.

We are living in times
that are both difficult to navigate
and to recount.
They present a
challenge for all of us,
but it is one that we should not
run away from.
On the contrary,
they demand that each one of us,
in our different roles and services,
never give in to mediocrity.

We are followers of Christ.
Christ goes before us.
The world needs his light.

Humanity needs him [Christ]
as the bridge
that can lead us to God and his love.

Help us, one and all,
to build bridges
through dialogue and encounter,
joining together as one people,
always at peace.

We must look for ways
to be a missionary Church,
a Church that builds bridges
and encourages dialogue,
a Church ever open to welcoming . . .
all those who are in need
of our charity, our presence,
our readiness to dialogue,
and our love.

We want to be a synodal Church,
a Church that moves forward,
a Church that always seeks peace,
that always seeks charity,
that always seeks to be close
above all to those who are suffering.

Together, as one people,
as brothers and sisters,
let us walk towards God
and love one another.

I, too,
express my affection for you
and my desire to share with you,
on our journey together,
our joys and sorrows,
our struggles and hopes.

For my part,
I would like to express
my firm desire . . .
to listen to everyone
as much as possible,
in order to learn, understand,
and decide things together.

Let us ask the Lord
for the grace to cultivate
and spread his charity,
and to become true neighbors
to one another. . . .
Let us compete in
showing the love that,
following his encounter with Christ,
drove the former persecutor
to become
"all things to all people"
(cf. 1 Cor 9:19-23),
even to the point of martyrdom.

Each person
can be a builder of unity
with his attitudes towards colleagues,
overcoming inevitable
misunderstandings with patience,
with humility, putting himself
in the shoes of others,
avoiding prejudices,
and also with a good dose of humor,
as Pope Francis taught us.

Love and unity:
These are the two dimensions
of the mission entrusted
to Peter by Jesus.

I trust that God's providence
will allow me further occasions
to get to know the countries
from which you come
and enable me
to have occasions to
confirm in the faith
our many brothers and sisters
throughout the world
and to build new bridges
with all people of good will.

Beginning with Saint Peter
and up to myself,
his unworthy Successor,
the pope has been a
humble servant of God
and of his brothers and sisters,
and nothing more than this.

The ministry of Peter is distinguished precisely by this self-sacrificing love, because the Church of Rome presides in charity, and its true authority is the charity of Christ. It is never a question of capturing others by force, by religious propaganda, or by means of power. Instead, it is always and only a question of loving as Jesus did.

If the rock is Christ,
Peter must shepherd the flock
without ever yielding to the temptation
to be an autocrat,
lording it over those entrusted to him
(cf. 1 Pet 5:3).

Popes pass; the Curia remains.
This applies to
every particular Church,
for the episcopal Curias.
And it also applies to the Curia
of the Bishop of Rome.

The Curia is the institution
that preserves and transmits
the historical memory of a Church,
of the ministry of its bishops.

* * *

Memory is an essential element in a living organism. It is not only directed to the past but nourishes the present and guides the future. Without memory, the path is lost; it loses its sense of direction.

We *remember*, that is,
we reflect in our hearts
upon what we have
experienced and learned,
in order to understand more fully
its meaning and to savor its beauty.

It is up to us to be docile listeners to his voice and faithful ministers of his plan of salvation, mindful that God loves to communicate himself, not in the roar of thunder and earthquakes, but in the "whisper of a gentle breeze" (1 Kings 19:12) or, as some translate it, in a "sound of sheer silence." It is this essential and important encounter to which we must guide and accompany all the holy People of God entrusted to our care.

I would like that our first great desire
be for a united Church,
a sign of unity and communion,
which becomes a leaven
for a reconciled world.

In this, our time, we still see too much discord, too many wounds caused by hatred, violence, prejudice, the fear of difference, and an economic paradigm that exploits the Earth's resources and marginalizes the poorest. For our part, we want to be a small leaven of unity, communion, and fraternity within the world.

As Bishop of Rome,
I consider one of my priorities
to be that of seeking
the re-establishment
of full and visible communion
among all those who profess
the same faith in God the Father,
the Son, and the Holy Spirit.

Our communion is realized to the extent that we meet in the Lord Jesus. The more faithful and obedient we are to him, the more united we are among ourselves. We Christians, then, are all called to pray and work together to reach this goal, step by step, which is and remains the work of the Holy Spirit.

Our common path
can and must also be understood
in the broad sense
of involving everyone,
in the spirit of human fraternity
that I mentioned above.

Now is the time for dialogue
and building bridges.

I am convinced that if we are in agreement and free from ideological and political conditioning, we can be effective in saying "no" to war and "yes" to peace, "no" to the arms race and "yes" to disarmament, "no" to an economy that impoverishes peoples and the Earth, and "yes" to integral development.

We want to say to the world, with humility and joy: Look to Christ! Come closer to him! Welcome his word that enlightens and consoles! Listen to his offer of love and become his one family:

In the one Christ, we are one.

This is the path to follow together, among ourselves but also with our sister Christian churches, with those who follow other religious paths, with those who are searching for God, with all women and men of good will, in order to build a new world where peace reigns!

This is the missionary spirit
that must animate us:
not closing ourselves off
in our small groups,
nor feeling superior to the world.
We are called
to offer God's love to everyone
in order to achieve that unity
which does not cancel out differences
but values the personal history
of each person and the social
and religious culture of every people.

In his mercy,
God has always desired
to draw all people to himself.
It is his life,
bestowed upon us in Christ,
that makes us one,
uniting us with one another.

As soon as we were born,
we needed others in order to live;
left to ourselves,
we would not have survived.
Someone else saved us
by caring for us in body and spirit.
All of us are alive today
thanks to a relationship,
a free and freeing relationship
of human kindness and mutual care.

When will we, too, be capable of interrupting our journey and having compassion? When we understand that the wounded man in the street represents each one of us. And then the memory of all the times that Jesus stopped to take care of us will make us more capable of compassion.

God is not solitary.
God, as Father, Son, and Holy Spirit,
is a "with" in himself,
and God with us.

In him, God,
in order to make himself
close and accessible
to men and women,
revealed himself to us
in the trusting eyes of a child,
in the lively mind of a young person,
and in the mature features of a man.

We are a people on the move.
This does not set us apart
but unites us to humanity,
like the yeast in a mass of dough,
which causes it to rise.

In a divided and troubled world,
the Holy Spirit teaches us
to walk together in unity.
The earth will rest, justice will prevail,
the poor will rejoice,
and peace will return,
once we no longer act as predators
but as pilgrims.
No longer each of us for ourselves,
but walking alongside one another.

The Spirit
broadens the borders
of our relationships
and opens us to the joy of fraternity.
This is also a critical yardstick
for the Church.
For we are truly the Church
of the Risen Lord
and disciples of Pentecost
if there are no borders
or divisions among us,
if we are able to dialogue
and accept one another in the Church,
and to reconcile our diversities,
and if, as Church, we become a
welcoming and hospitable place for all.

The Spirit breaks down barriers and tears down the walls of indifference and hatred because he "teaches us all things" and "reminds us of Jesus' words" (cf. Jn 14:26). He teaches us, reminds us, and writes in our hearts before all else the commandment of love that the Lord has made the center and summit of everything.

Where there is love,
there is no room for prejudice,
for "security" zones separating us
from our neighbors,
for the exclusionary mindset
that, tragically, we now see emerging
also in political nationalisms.

All creation exists
solely in the form of coexistence,
sometimes dangerous,
yet always interconnected.

In our dialogue,
I would like us always to preserve
the sense of being a family.
Indeed, the diplomatic community
represents the entire
family of peoples,
a family that shares the
joys and sorrows of life
and the human and spiritual values
that give it meaning and direction.

Let us not forget:
Families are the cradle
of the future of humanity.

With a heart
filled with gratitude and hope,
I would remind all married couples
that marriage is not an ideal
but the measure of true love
between a man and a woman:
a love that is total, faithful,
and fruitful.

Finally, dear grandparents
and elderly people,
I recommend that you watch
over your loved ones
with wisdom and compassion
and with the humility
and patience
that come with age.

Families . . .
are small domestic churches
where the message of the Gospel
is received and passed on.

In the family,
faith is handed on
together with life,
generation after generation.
It is shared like food
at the family table
and like the love in our hearts.
In this way,
families become privileged places
in which to encounter Jesus,
who loves us and
desires our good, always.

In this promotion
of the common good,
our social responsibility is grounded
in God's creative act,
which gives everyone a share
in the goods of the earth.

Like those goods,
the fruits of human labor
should be equally accessible to all.

Helping the poor
is a matter of justice
before [being] a question of charity.

The poor are not a distraction for the Church but our beloved brothers and sisters, for by their lives, their words, and their wisdom, they put us in contact with the truth of the Gospel.

* * *

The poor are not recipients
of our pastoral care,
but creative subjects
who challenge us to find novel ways
of living out the Gospel today.

The poor can be witnesses to a strong and steadfast hope precisely because they embody it in the midst of uncertainty, poverty, instability, and marginalization. They cannot rely on the security of power and possessions; on the contrary, they are at their mercy and often victims of them. Their hope must necessarily be sought elsewhere.

Once we desire
that God accompany us
on the journey of life,
material wealth becomes relativized,
for we discover the real treasure
that we need.

* * *

The gravest form of poverty
is not to know God.

All this earth's goods, material realities, worldly pleasures, economic prosperity, however important, cannot bring happiness to our hearts. Wealth often disappoints and can lead to tragic situations of poverty—above all, the poverty born of the failure to recognize our need for God and of the attempt to live without him.

Truly peaceful relationships
cannot be built . . .
apart from truth.

Truth
can never be separated
from charity,
which always has at its root
a concern for the life
and well-being of every
man and woman.

From the Christian perspective,
truth is not the affirmation
of abstract and
disembodied principles,
but an encounter
with the person of Christ himself,
alive in the midst
of the community of believers.

The Church can never be exempted
from speaking the truth
about humanity and the world,
resorting whenever necessary
to blunt language that may
initially create misunderstanding.

Truth,

then, does not create division,
but rather enables us
to confront all the more resolutely
the challenges of our time,
such as migration,
the ethical use
of artificial intelligence,
and the protection
of our beloved planet Earth.

These are challenges
that require commitment
and cooperation on the part of all,
since no one can think
of facing them alone.

It is a time of conversion and renewal and, above all, an opportunity to leave conflicts behind and embark on a new path, confident that, by working together, each of us, in accordance with his or her own sensibilities and responsibilities, can build a world in which everyone can lead an authentically human life in truth, justice, and peace.

It is my hope that this will be the case everywhere.

Where words take on ambiguous and ambivalent connotations, and the virtual world, with its altered perception of reality, takes over unchecked, it is difficult to build authentic relationships, since the objective and real premises of communication are lacking.

Communication is not only
the transmission of information,
but it is also the creation of a culture,
of human and digital environments
that become spaces for dialogue
and discussion.

The Church . . . recognizes in [imprisoned journalists] the courage of those who defend dignity, justice, and the right of people to be informed, because only informed individuals can make free choices.

There is so little dialogue around us; shouting often replaces it, not infrequently in the form of fake news and irrational arguments proposed by a few loud voices. Deeper reflection and study are essential, as well as a commitment to encounter and listen to the poor, who are a treasure for the Church and for humanity. Their viewpoints, though often disregarded, are vital if we are to see the world through God's eyes.

In our own day,
the Church offers to everyone
the treasury of her social teaching
in response to
another industrial revolution
and to developments in the field
of artificial intelligence
that pose new challenges
for the defense of human dignity,
justice, and labor.

The challenges facing humanity
will be less frightening,
the future will be less dark,
and discernment will be
less complicated . . .
if together we obey the Holy Spirit!

The Spirit opens borders, first of all, in our hearts. He is the Gift that opens our lives to love. His presence breaks down our hardness of heart, our narrowness of mind, our selfishness, the fears that enchain us, and the narcissism that makes us think only of ourselves.

The Spirit of God . . . puts us in touch with our inmost self, beneath all the masks we wear. He leads us to an encounter with the Lord by teaching us to experience the joy that is his gift. He convinces us, as we just heard in Jesus' words, that only by abiding in love will we receive the strength to remain faithful to his word and to let it transform us. The Spirit opens our interior borders, so that our lives can become places of welcome and refreshment.

Salvation
does not come about by magic
but by a mysterious interplay
of *grace* and *faith*,
of God's prevenient love
and of our trusting and
free acceptance (cf. 2 Tim 1:12).

God is confident and hopes that sooner or later the seed will blossom. This is how he loves us: He does not wait for us to become the best soil, but he always generously gives us his word. Perhaps by seeing that he trusts us, the desire to be better soil will be kindled in us. This is hope founded on the rock of God's generosity and mercy.

Even when it seems
we are able to do little in life,
it is always worthwhile.
There is always the possibility
to find meaning
because God loves our life.

I would like to say,
especially to the young,
do not wait,
but respond enthusiastically
to the Lord who calls us to work
in his vineyard.
Do not delay; roll up your sleeves,
because the Lord is generous
and you will not be disappointed!

It is important that young men and women on their vocational journey find *acceptance*, *listening*, and *encouragement* in their communities and that they can look up to credible models of generous dedication to God and to their brothers and sisters.

Jesus
does not establish rankings;
he gives all of himself to those
who open their hearts to him.

If we remain in his love,
he comes to dwell in us,
and our life will become
a temple of God.
His love enlightens us,
influences the way we think
and act, spreads outwards to others,
and embraces every situation
in our lives.

This dwelling of God within us, brothers and sisters, is precisely the gift of the Holy Spirit, who takes us by the hand and enables us to experience God's presence and closeness amid our daily lives, for he makes us his home.

This is the hour for love!
The heart of the Gospel
is the love of God
that makes us brothers and sisters.

The Spirit of Jesus
changes the world
because he changes hearts.

The Spirit inspires the contemplative dimension of life that rejects self-assertion, complaining, rivalry, and the temptation to control consciences and resources. The Lord is the Spirit, and where the Spirit of the Lord is, there is freedom (cf. 2 Cor 3:17).

Evangelization, dear brothers and sisters, is not our attempt to conquer the world, but the infinite grace that radiates from lives transformed by the Kingdom of God. It is the way of the Beatitudes, a path that we tread together, between the "already" and the "not yet," hungering and thirsting for justice, poor in spirit, merciful, meek, pure of heart, men and women of peace.

An authentic spirituality
commits us to
integral human development,
to making Jesus' words
a reality in our lives.
When this happens,
there is always joy.
—Joy and hope.

The word of God
tells us that Christian hope
is certainty at every step
of life's journey,
since it does not depend
on our human strength
but upon the promise of God,
who is always faithful.

Christian hope
is like an anchor
that grounds our hearts
in the promise of the Lord Jesus,
who saved us by his death
and resurrection
and will come again among us.

Hope is born of faith, which nourishes and sustains it on the foundation of charity, the mother of all virtues. All of us need charity, here and now. Charity is not just a promise; it is a present reality to be embraced with joy and responsibility. Charity engages us and guides our decisions towards the common good.

Conversely, those who lack charity not only lack faith and hope; they also rob their neighbors of hope.

Amid life's trials,
our hope is inspired
by the firm and reassuring certainty
of God's love,
poured into our hearts
by the Holy Spirit.
That hope does not disappoint
(cf. Rom 5:5).

By recognizing
that God is our first and only hope,
we too pass from fleeting *hopes*
to a lasting *hope.*

It is up to them [the disciples] to carry on this mission, to cast their nets again and again, to bring the hope of the Gospel into the "waters" of the world, to sail the seas of life so that all may experience God's embrace.

All of us are in God's hands.
So, let us move forward,
without fear, together,
hand in hand with God
and with one another!

Significant Dates and Events

1955–September 14: Birth of Robert Francis Prevost, in Chicago. His father, Louis Marius Prevost, is of French and Italian descent, while his mother, Mildred Martinez, has Spanish and Creole roots. Robert grows up with his brothers Louis Martin and John Joseph.

1973–High school graduation from the Saint Augustine Seminary in Michigan. Begins studying mathematics and philosophy at Villanova University, in Philadelphia.

1977–Completes requirements for degrees in both mathematics and philosophy.

1977–September 1: Entrance into the Augustinian Order; beginning of novitiate in St. Louis in the Province of Mother of Good Counsel, in Chicago.

1978–September 2: First profession and theological studies at the Catholic Theological Union, in Chicago.

1981–August 29: Perpetual profession and completion of theological studies; further studies in Rome at the Pontifical University of St. Thomas Aquinas (Angelicum) in the field of canon law.

1982–June 19: Ordination as a priest at the Roman Augustinian College of Santa Monica, by Belgian Archbishop Jean Jadot, then Vice President of the Pontifical Council for Non-Christians.

1985–Move to Peru and work at the Augustinian mission in Chulucanas, Piura, while preparing for his doctorate.

1987–Doctorate in canon law with a thesis on "The Role of the Local Prior of the Augustinian Order"; appointed Director of Vocations and Mission Director of the Augustinian Province Mother of Good Counsel, in Olympia Fields, Illinois.

1988–Returned to Peru, joining the mission in Trujillo; head of the joint training project for Augustinian candidates from the vicariates of Chulucanas, Iquitos, and Apurímac. For eleven years, Fr. Prevost is prior of the community (1988–1992), director of formation (1988–1998) and teacher of the professed

(1992–1998), as well as judicial vicar in the Archdiocese of Trujillo (1989–1998) and professor of canon law, patristics, and moral theology at the Seminar San Carlos y San Marcelo. At the same time, he is entrusted with the pastoral care of the parish of Our Lady, Mother of the Church, later named St. Rita (1988–1999), in a poor suburb of the city.

1992 to 1999–He also worked as administrator of the parish of Our Lady of Monserrat, also in Trujillo.

1999 to 2001–Provincial Superior of the Augustinian Province Mother of Good Counsel, in Chicago.

2001 to 2013–Prior General of the Augustinian Order, based in Rome.

2013–October 2: Return to the Augustinian Province of Chicago, where Fr. Prevost initially served as director of formation at the local monastery and at the same time as first councilor and provincial vicar.

2014–November 3: Appointed Apostolic administrator of the Peruvian diocese of Chiclayo by Pope Francis.

2014–December 12: Episcopal consecration, in St. Mary's Cathedral. He uses the words "In illo uno unum" by St. Augustine as his episcopal motto (cf. above, p. xvii).

2015–August 24: Acquisition of (additional) Peruvian citizenship.

2015–September 26: Appointment by Pope Francis as Diocesan Bishop of Chiclayo.

2018–In the Peruvian Bishops' Conference, Bishop Prevost serves as vice president (since March 2018) and chairman of the Commission for Education and Culture, as well as a member of the Economic Council.

2019–July 13: Appointed by Pope Francis as a member of the Congregation for the Clergy.

2020–April 15: Appointed by Pope Francis as Apostolic Administrator of the Peruvian Diocese of Callao.

2020–November 21: Appointed by Pope Francis as a member of the Congregation for Bishops.

2023–January 30: Appointed by Pope Francis as Prefect of the Dicastery for

Bishops and President of the Pontifical Commission for Latin America; elevated to Archbishop.

2023–September 30: Elevated by Pope Francis to Cardinal Deacon with the Roman titular church of Santa Monica.

2023–October 4: Appointed by Pope Francis as member of the Dicastery for Evangelization (Section for New Evangelization and New Churches), the Dicastery for the Doctrine of the Faith, the Dicastery for the Oriental Churches, the Dicastery for the Clergy, the Dicastery for Institutes of Consecrated Life and Societies of Apostolic Life, the Dicastery for Culture and Education, the Dicastery for Legislative Texts, and as a member of the Pontifical Commission for the Vatican City State.

2023–October 4 to 29: Member of the World Synod on the theme "For a Synodal Church: Communion, Participation, Mission" (first session).

2024–October 2 to 27: Member of the World Synod on the theme "For a Synodal Church: Communion, Participation, Mission" (second session).

2025–February 6: Elevation to Cardinal Bishop of the Suburbicarian Diocese of Albano.

2025–May 7: Start of the conclave to elect the successor to Pope Francis.

2025–May 8: Election of Cardinal Robert Francis Prevost as the 267th Bishop of Rome and Pope, who takes the name Leo XIV.

2025–May 18: Inauguration in St. Peter's Square.

Coat of Arms

Pope Leo XIV chose for his coat of arms the images that already adorned his cardinal's coat of arms, now supplemented by the papal symbols. It is divided diagonally to the left, with an upper blue field—a color that refers to the sky and carries Marian symbolism—in which a white lily can be seen: a classic sign of veneration of the Blessed Virgin Mary (*flos florum*—flower of flowers). The lower ivory field shows the emblem of the Augustinian Order: a flaming heart pierced by an arrow, resting on a closed natural-colored book.

This depiction symbolizes the words of St. Augustine, such as: "*Sagittaveras tu cor meum charitate tua*"— "You have pierced my heart with your love," or also "*Vulnerasti cor meum verbo tuo*"— "You have pierced my heart with your word" —different formulations of the same spiritual experience.

Since the sixteenth century, this symbol has been an integral part of the Augustinian coat of arms—with various designs, usually resting on a book symbolizing the Word of God, which can transform a person's heart—as it did with Augustine himself. The book also refers to the brilliant spiritual work that the Church Father gave to the Church and to humanity. The color white (here ivory) is a symbol of holiness and purity and is also found in other religious coats of arms. The coat of arms is surmounted by the symbols of papal dignity: a silver miter adorned with three golden bands, alluding to the historical tiara, and the crossed keys of St. Peter—the right key is gold, the left key is silver—held together by a red cord.

Pope Leo XIV continues to use his episcopal motto ("In Illo uno unum"— "In the One [= Christ], we are one") as his motto.

Sources

The numbers in parentheses correspond to the sayings in this anthology.

Address to the College of Cardinals, Synodal Hall, May 10, 2025 (30, 36, 78).

Address to Members of the "*Centesimus Annus Pro Pontifice*" Foundation, Clementine Hall, May 17, 2025 (77).

Address to Representatives of Other Churches and Ecclesial Communities, and Other Religions, Clementine Hall, May 19, 2025 (39–42).

Address to Representatives of the Media, Audience Hall, May 12, 2025 (11–13, 16, 18, 75f).

Address to Superiors and Officials of the Secretariat of State, Clementine Hall, June 5, 2025 (17).

Address to the Movements and Associations of the "Arena of Peace" (Verona), May 30, 2025 (4b–7).

Angelus, May 25, 2025 (88f); June 1, 2025 (60).

Audience with Members of the Diplomatic Corps Accredited to the Holy See, Clementine Hall, May 16, 2025 (3, 4a, 8, 10, 14f, 29, 56, 68–74).

First Apostolic Blessing *"Urbi et Orbi,"* Central Loggia of the Vatican Basilica, May 8, 2025 (1f, 19–22, 100).

General Audience, St. Peter's Square, May 21, 2025 (83); May 28, 2025 (47); June 4, 2025 (84f, 87).

Homily for the Holy Mass for the Beginning of the Pontificate of Pope Leo XIV, Saint Peter's Square, May 18, 2025 (23, 28, 31f, 37f, 43f, 90, 99).

Homily for the Holy Mass on the Solemnity of Pentecost: Jubilee of Movements, Associations and New Communities, St. Peter's Square, June 8, 2025 (52–54, 80f).

Homily for the Holy Mass *Pro Ecclesia* Celebrated by the Roman Pontiff with the Cardinals, Sistine Chapel, May 9, 2025 (49).

Homily for the Holy Mass with Presbyteral Ordinations, Saint Peter's Basilica, May 31, 2025 (45f, 57–59).

Homily for the Mass for the Jubilee of Families, Children, Grandparents and the Elderly, St. Peter's Square, June 1, 2025 (61).

Homily for the Papal Mass for the Possession of the Chair of the Bishop of Rome, Lateran Basilica, May 25, 2025 (24f, 35).

Homily for the Vigil of Pentecost, St. Peter's Square, June 7, 2025 (48, 50f, 55, 79, 91–93).

Homily for the Visit to the Tomb of Saint Paul, Basilica of Saint Paul Outside the Walls, May 20, 2025 (26, 82).

Meeting of the Holy Father with Employees of the Holy See and the Vatican City State, Audience Hall, May 24, 2025 (27, 33f).

Message for the 9th World Day of the Poor, June 13, 2025 (62–67, 94–98).

Regina Caeli, Loggia of the Blessings of St. Peter's Basilica, May 11, 2025 (86); June 8, 2025 (9).

www.ingramcontent.com/pod-product-compliance
Lightning Source LLC
LaVergne TN
LVHW020637100826
845148LV00012B/2215

* 9 7 8 1 5 6 5 4 8 7 3 2 1 *